Blew

and

the Death of the Mag

by

Wendy Lichtman

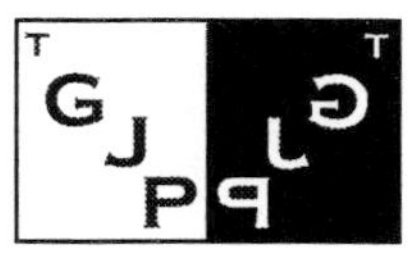

A Publication of The Gestalt Journal Press

Published by:

THE GESTALT JOURNAL PRESS
A Division of The Center for Gestalt Development
P.O. Box 990
Highland, NY 12528

With illustrations by Diane Mayers

This book was originally published by Freestone Publishing Co. in 1975.

ISBN 0939266-35-0 (Hardcover)
ISBN 0939266-34-2 (Softcover)

*T*his is a story about death,

    the death of the Magnafantagna.

It is also about Blew,

    the girl who loved the Magnafantagna.

Blew was having a hard time describing the
Magnafantagna. Even Blew's good friend Shane,
who usually understood everything
very quickly, didn't understand this.

"What's that word you're saying?" Shane asked.

"Mag-na-fan-tag-na," Blew said, slowly.
"But sometimes I just call her 'Mag.' You see,"
Blew explained, "my Magnafantagna does two
special things. She *magnifies* what's happening,
and she makes everything *fantastic!*
Magnafantagna!"

"What do you mean she *magnifies* what's happening?" Shane asked.

"I mean," Blew said, "that the Mag makes things so I can see them better, and feel them more. She finds the special part of everything I do, and helps me find it too."

"Oh," Shane said, "like flattery.
My brother does that. Yesterday
he said, 'You wash dishes better and
faster than anyone, and you never
argue over doing extra chores.' I felt real
smart and nice, so even though it was his
turn to do the dishes, I washed them. But
after the job was done I knew I had been
tricked, because I did all the work, and all
he did was flatter." Shane shook her head.
"I don't like flattery," she said.

Blew sighed. "That's not like the
Magnafantagna. She doesn't flatter
or trick me. She doesn't want me to act
any particular way. She doesn't want
anything from me. She just...is."

"Well, that's good," Shane smiled.
"What does she look like, Blew?"

"She's kind of see-through," Blew answered.
"But she has a bright glow. She's real lively,
and she's warm to be near."

As Blew spoke about the Magnafantagna,
she looked bright and lively and warm
to be near too.

"The Mag sounds beautiful," Shane said.
And then she whispered,

> "Is she real, Blew?
> I mean *really* real?"

"Oh yes, Shane. Very real. When the Magnafantagna isn't around, everything seems plain."

"But when I'm with her it's different. Everything is magnified. Everything is made fantastic!"

"You know that trapeze that hangs from the tree?" Blew asked. "Well, the other day when I played on it, the Mag was with me, and it sure didn't feel like I was swinging then. I felt like I was *flying!*"

Blew remembered how she had grabbed hold of the bar and run back and forth to build up speed. Then she'd swung her feet right up to the top, wrapping them around the ropes.

"What a fine take-off!"
exclaimed the Magnafantagna.

Blew had lifted up her head and watched as she glided through the air, feeling the wind rush past her.

"A beautiful flight — you are a magnificent bird!"

Blew hadn't wanted to lose her grip. She'd lowered her feet to slow down.

"What fine control — what a gentle descent!"

Her feet had touched the ground, the trip safely finished.

"A perfect landing!"

Blew's heart was beating fast; her face felt hot.

She was so excited to have been *flying*!

Blew had other experiences with the Mag that
she didn't tell anybody about, not even Shane.
Like the time she looked in the mirror and felt
disappointed. "Brown eyes," Blew thought,
"plain brown eyes."

But when she heard the Mag's voice,
it all seemed different.

*"Sparkling almond-shaped eyes. When you
laugh, your eyes twinkle. The sides turn up and
join your bright smile.*

*When you cry, those eyes fill with tears like a
soft, sad puppy dog.*

*When you are
angry, your eyes
narrow, getting
fiery and sharp."*

Blew listened intently,
amazed that the Mag
could see so much.

*"When you're silly and mischievous, your eyes
dance quickly back and forth.*

*And when you're attentive and trusting like
now, your eyes are wide open, bright and clear.*

*Eyes that show feeling,
eyes that show intelligence,
    beautiful, sparkling
      brown eyes."*

How could all that be in my eyes, Blew
wondered. But darting a glance back
    in the mirror, there they were –
    beautiful, sparkling,
      brown eyes.

And so Blew learned that her feelings were
shown in her eyes. This pleased her.

But she also wondered about something that
didn't please her. Could it be that the
Magnafantagna could see and magnify
feelings even when Blew didn't want her to?

Some feelings, thought Blew, are just mine.
I don't want them magnified. I don't want them
made fantastic. I don't want them changed. So
Blew made her eyelids flop over her eyes when
the private feelings came.

This, she thought, would keep them her own.

There were some other complicated things about
feelings that Blew was coming to understand with
the Magnafantagna.

Blew like to sew, and she wanted to make the
Mag a patchwork quilt. She carefully chose
many pieces of material and took special time
and effort to arrange them. Then she sewed
them all together and was delighted. The quilt
was beautiful!

She was excited to give it to the Magnafantagna.
Then it would be even more beautiful. It would
be a *masterpiece!*

Blew looked forward to seeing the Mag smile,
and to hearing her comment on every patch and
every stitch.

But the reaction was quite different.

When Blew gave her the gift, the Magnafantagna
didn't say a word.
She just held the beautiful quilt
close to her, and quietly cried.

Blew was surprised.

Didn't the Mag *like* her gift?
Why didn't she say anything?

But soon Blew sat quietly with tears
in her eyes, too.

    She began to understand that
    the magnification of words is
    is sometimes *silence*,

    and the magnification of
    joy is sometimes *tears*.

$\mathcal{M}$ainly, life with the Magnafantagna was
very special and very happy. It went on
like this for a long time. Blew thought it
would always be this way.

Very slowly though, Blew began noticing
that things seemed different.

The Magnafantagna wasn't around as
often, and Blew wondered why.

When they were together, the Mag felt
softer and quieter. It was like being with
a gentle cloud.

Then Blew got scared, fearing the Mag was sick!

She remembered when her grandfather had
been sick. The doctor had checked him, done
some tests, and come out with the awful news
that Grandpa was dying.

> Blew's heart started
> beating very fast,
> her throat tightened,
> her eyes got full of tears
> and her hands got shaky.

Was the Mag sick?
Blew was very frightened.

The days passed slowly.

Often Blew sat by the window,
but she didn't see much,
and she didn't say much.

Blew knew what the doctor had said about
her grandfather, and she was afraid to hear
those words about the Mag.

    "The news is not good.
    This very lovely, very
    special Magnafantagna
    is terribly sick. She will
    probably not live long.
    I'm sorry."

NO!

It isn't true, thought Blew.
It can't be true.
Those doctors are wrong,
        or stupid,
        or both.

Or if, by chance, they're right,
the Magnafantagna is different.
        She will get better!
        She is special!
        She is mine!
        She won't die!

NO!

Not now, not soon!
There's so much more I need to see   *magnified*,
so much more that needs to be *fantastic!* My
Mag has to live a long time. She must. That's
all there is to it!

So Blew decided that the Magnafantagna
wouldn't die.

She tried not to notice that the Mag
didn't glow as much. And she told
herself that it was just fine that the
Mag felt like being a little quieter.

It took a long time for Blew to admit that the
decision wasn't hers to make.

Blew didn't know who it was who *did* decide
who died, and when, but it sure wasn't *her*.

"Who decides about death?"
Blew asked everyone.

Shane didn't know either. She shrugged her
shoulders, shook her head, and looked down.

Blew's aunt said it was God who decided. She said that Blew could pray and ask God that the death be peaceful, and that she be given strength during this time.

But Blew didn't pray for that.
Instead, she tried to explain to God that the decision was a mistake. She pleaded that it be changed and that the Mag be all better.

Blew's father said that life went up and down like ocean waves, and the death, like birth, was one of those waves.

That didn't seem right to Blew. She remembered her dog giving birth. That was wonderful, with fuzzy puppies where there had been none before. No, death was not at all like birth.

Blew's brother said, "I don't like talking about it, Blew. Just stop!"

Nobody could help.
She felt very alone,
and very afraid.

She wanted to ask the Magnafantagna,
but she didn't ask her. Blew was afraid
she would have to learn to do everything
without the Mag soon, so she thought she
had better start now.

Besides, Blew was afraid to show fear in
front of the Mag. She was afraid that the
fear would be made even bigger and even
scarier. So Blew pretended that she wasn't
afraid of anything.

> She flopped her eyelids over her eyes,
> she stood up very straight, and she used
> big, strong words when she spoke.

Then Blew felt angry at the Magnafantagna
because she had to cover up her fear.

> Blew wasn't only afraid about the
> Mag's death, she was also afraid to
> show her fear of the death. That
> made it twice as bad.

Blew felt angry too, that the Magnafantagna
was dying and leaving her before she got
the courage to show the fear and look at it
with her.

She was angry at the Mag for dying before
everything was looked at, before everything
was understood.

How could she ever do it alone?

Blew was angry at many other things, too.

She was angry at her family, her friends,
and the doctors. Sometimes the anger
seemed right to her, and sometimes the
anger didn't seem right, but she still felt it.

Blew said some mean things then. "If
something has to die," she asked Shane,
"why can't it be your stupid pet snake?
He's not nearly as good as the Magnafantagna.
He doesn't *magnify*. He doesn't make
anything *fantastic*. As far as I can tell, the best
thing he can do is wiggle."

Shane felt bad. She felt angry at Blew for
saying such a mean thing, and she wanted
to get back at her. Shane was about to say
that she knew Blew cheated at chess, and
she hated it when Blew tickled her

　　　　　　　but something stopped her.

Maybe it was Blew's eyes.

They looked sad and scared.

So Shane forgot about the chess game and
the tickling, and said, "I know you're feeling
real bad, Blew."

Blew signed a deep breath, hugged her good
friend, and said very softly,

"It's so unfair, Shane."

Then Blew started playing the *If only*
game with herself.

    If only I hadn't given her so much to
          magnify and make fantastic,
          maybe she'd be well.

    If only I hadn't ever yelled at her, maybe
          she wouldn't have gotten sick.

    If only she lives to my next birthday,
          I'll be happy.

    If only she gets better, I'll never hurt
          anybody ever.

    If only she gets well, I'll become a doctor,
          and never let anyone die.

    If only she lives, I'll never do anything
          wrong again.

Blew felt very confused.

Sometimes she thought she knew a lot.
Sometimes she thought she didn't know
anything.

Blew knew that the death was coming soon,

> but she still hoped that the
>
> death wouldn't come at all.

She knew she wanted to hide her sadness
and fear from the Magnafantagna,

> but she also wanted to be able
>
> to show it and talk about it.

She tried to make herself flop her eyelids
over her eyes, she tried to make herself smile,

> but her eyes filled with tears,
>
> her soft voice cracked, and
>
> she swallowed a lot.

The Magnafantagna saw all this.

One day, the Magnafantagna said,
"It's time for us to talk, Blew."

The Mag's serious voice scared Blew.
She tightened her hands in fists around
her thumbs.

She would rather have skipped the talking
now. But the Mag was right. It was time for
them to talk.

The Magnafantagna was having a lot of
feelings too, maybe even more than Blew;
after all, she was the one who was so sick.

They spoke of what they knew and of what
they didn't know.

They spoke of the sadnesses they knew,
        of pets dying,
        of seeing a small animal hurt,
        of watching the sick get sicker,
        of missing the ones you love,
        of not being around for joyful times,
        of not seeing beautiful things.

They didn't know how to put it all in words, so
sometimes they just touched.

They spoke of the scariest fears they knew,

>of hearing a strange noise in the dark,

>of falling off things,

>of getting lost,

>of being left alone,

>of pain,

>of dying.

The most frightening thing, they both agreed,
was *not knowing* exactly what the fear was about.

Blew felt her hands still in fists. She
was holding on tightly to her thumbs.
It was hard to talk like this.

Blew and the Mag really didn't know what
would be coming.

It did feel better, though, to share the
unknowing with each other.

There were some things they did know for
sure, and they talked about those, too.

> They knew about all their wonderful
> memories, and their fine times
> together, and they laughed about
> some of them,

> and Blew knew a secret about her
> cousin's best friend's sister, and she
> told that.

They even said the things that they knew
the other one knew, too.

But they said it anyway. They said,
      "I love you, Mag."
      "I love you, Blew."

And then Blew finally let go of her
thumbs. She felt her small hands relax
and open.

Then one day very quietly

the Magnafantagna died.

Blew sat down, hurting all over,

and cried, and cried,

and cried.

*A*fter the Magnafantagna's death, Blew
was surprised that other people thought
things were the same as before.

The buses were still running.
People were still going to work
and school and picnics.
Shane's snake was still wiggling.

Things sure weren't the same for Blew.

In the days that followed, Blew felt a pain
she had never known before.

It was as though all the beauty and fun
and specialness that ever existed had gone.

It was as though the world had no colors,
just gray, black, and white.

It was as though nothing mattered.
Everything seemed stupid, and
unimportant, and why bother?

Blew didn't want to see beauty that the
Magnafantagna couldn't share.

She didn't want to hear laughter that
the Magnafantagna wouldn't make
into a roar.

When she played on the trapeze, it sure
didn't feel like she was flying.
Her feet dragged on the ground and
her arms ached.

She felt so weak and heavy.
She missed the Mag so much.

The hurt didn't stop either — it just kept on.
Before, every other pain had soon ended.

When Blew fell off her bike, her leg had
bled, had been bandaged, and had healed,
                              and she felt better.

When everyone ran away from her when they
played hide and seek and she was "it," Blew always
felt lost. She tried to find the other people, but if
she couldn't, she'd call "ally-ally-in-come-free,"
and like magic they'd appear,
                              and she felt better.

Sometimes Blew would get very sad at sunsets.
But the morning always came, the sun always rose,
                              and she felt better.

This time she couldn't get herself to feel better.
She could only feel worse.

Sometimes Blew would dream of the
Magnafantagna, and wake up happy and
ready to do something fantastic with her.

But after a few moments awake, Blew
would remember that the Mag was gone,
and then she would hurt all over again.

When Blew went to the places alone where they
used to go together, she remembered the Mag and
missed her terribly.

But Blew wanted to go to those places,
even though the memories made her feel
sad, because to *not* remember made Blew
feel even sadder.

One day Blew walked to what had been
her favorite spot with the Magnafantagna,
a mountain that they would climb and,
from there, look at the world.

She got to the spot and looked for her
mountain. She couldn't find it. There was
only a small hill with a mole crawling out.

Of course, Blew realized with embarrassment
and sadness, without the Mag it's not a
beautiful mountain at all; it's just a dumb
molehill.

She almost laughed, but then she caught
herself. *"It's not funny!"* she yelled at the
mole, who really wasn't laughing anyway.

Blew stood on top of the small hill
and screamed out:

> *"Okay, it's time to end the hurt!*
>
> *The game is over!*
>
> *She can't be gone any more!*
>
> *Ally-ally-in-come-free!"*

Nobody appeared.

It was silent.

Blew looked at the mole to make sure he
still wasn't laughing at her for this outburst.

Certainly not.
He looked sad, and gentle, and very nice.

Then they sat together for a long time.

Each season that passed reminded Blew of
her loss.

In fall, when the leaves turned colors
and dropped from the trees, Blew
remembered how they had been last fall
when she was with the Magnafantagna.

In winter, the holidays passed quietly,
the first ones without the Mag.

Springtime brought the lilacs. New
flowers, new colors, and old memories
of how wonderful it had been to see
the beauty of other springs.

Blew was trying to understand her feelings about
death. They seemed connected, mysteriously, to
her feelings about life.

Life seemed different somehow, knowing
that death was real.

Sometimes when she wondered about these mysteries, Blew got a strange feeling that began in her stomach and ended as a chill at the back of her neck.

Blew didn't speak about this feeling with anyone else, though she thought that maybe other people got it too.

But maybe not.

It felt very private to her.

There were a lot of feelings that Blew *did*
want to talk about. She wanted to tell story
after story about the Mag,

> laughing at happy thoughts,
>
> crying at sad thoughts,
>
> thinking,
>
> remembering,
>
> talking.

Some people didn't want to hear what Blew felt.

> They wanted her to pretend everything
> was fine.
>
> They wanted her to stop speaking
> about death.
>
> They wanted her to stop thinking
> about the Mag.

Shane didn't want Blew to hide her feelings.

One rainy day when they were playing chess,
Blew told Shane about that time at the mirror. She
told her how the Mag had made her plain brown
eyes feel beautiful.

When Blew looked at Shane's eyes, they were
filled with tears.

"Is it okay to talk about her?" Blew asked.

Shane nodded.

"Really okay?" Blew checked. "You don't mind
crying?"

Shane shook her head. "It feels good to hear
the stories. My tears are kind of happy and
sad at the same time."

She understands, Blew thought.
Shane knows how I feel.

So Blew told Shane more. She even told
her about the large mountain that was
really a small mole hill, and the two of
them laughed and cried all at once.

Tears trickled down
past smiles.

Giggles and sobs got all
mixed up.

"With all these bright smiles and with all these
wet tears," Blew said, "my Mag would have
made a *rainbow!*"

Shane said, "Something strange happened to me the other day when I was playing on the trapeze, Blew. I remembered you telling me that when you were with the Magnafantagna you felt like you were flying when you used the trapeze. Well, just thinking about that, I got way up there, higher than ever before. It was wonderful! I'm sure I flew, too!"

"That is strange," Blew said. *"Very* strange."

Blew knew that Shane had just come back from visiting her grandparents and had flown in an airplane.

"Did it feel like flying in the airplane?" she asked.

"No. That's different. When I was in the
airplane, the airplane flew. I just sat inside it.
When I was on the trapeze, it felt like *I* flew."

Yes, that's it, thought Blew,
feeling the chill at the
back of her neck.

Shane spoke. "Hey, I almost forgot –
I've got a present for you."

Shane reached into her pocket and found
something the flight attendant had given
her on the plane. She handed it to Blew.
It was a pin shaped like wings, like the ones
pilots wear on their uniforms. Shane had
one for herself in the other pocket.

"For flying," she said quietly.

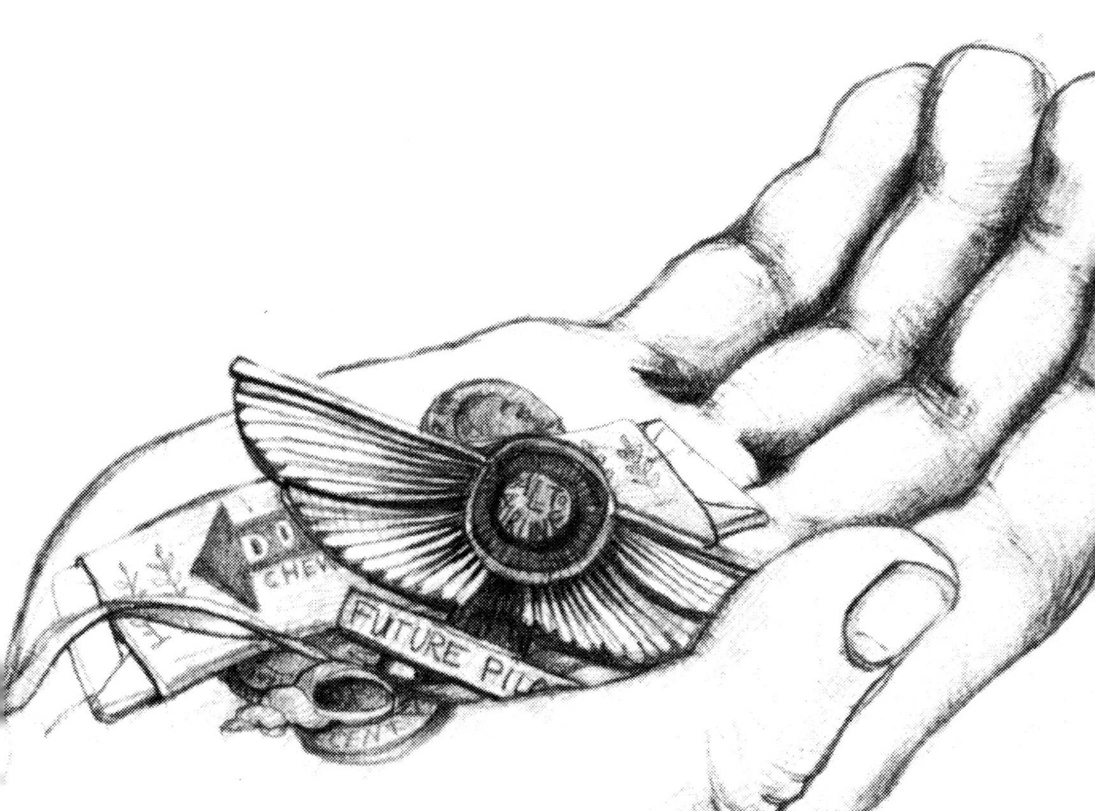

"Oh, Shane!"

No other words came.

Blew remembered what she had learned
from the Magnafantagna,

that the magnification of
words is sometimes *silence,*

and the magnification of
joy is sometimes *tears.*

The rain finally stopped. Blew and Shane
walked outside where it was sunny now.
They were both wearing their pilots' wings.

Blew looked up and saw it.
Right straight ahead was a *rainbow!*

She looked at Shane and started to smile,
feeling chills and warmth at the same time.